VILLAIN SONGS

VILLAIN SONGS

poems

TAMMY ROBACKER

MoonPathPress

Villain Songs, Second Edition
Copyright © 2018 Tammy Robacker

All rights reserved. No part of this publication may be reproduced
distributed or transmitted in any form or
by any means whatsoever without written permission
from the publisher, except in the case of brief excerpts
for critical reviews and articles.

All inquiries should be addressed to MoonPath Press.

Poetry
ISBN 978-1-936657-33-9

[First edition, 2017, published by ELJ Editions, Ltd., New York]

Author photo: Tammy Robacker

Cover Art: "The Sleeping Giant" by Courtney Carmody
(https://www.flickr.com/photos/calamity_photography/5173954692)

Design: Tonya Namura using LunchBox (display) & Athelas (text)

MoonPath Press is dedicated to publishing the finest poets of
the U.S. Pacific Northwest

MoonPath Press
PO Box 445
Tillamook, OR 97141

MoonPathPress@gmail.com

http://MoonPathPress.com

Acknowledgments

Some poems from the *Villain Songs* manuscript have been purposed in a poetry chapbook collection titled, *R* by Tammy Robacker. The chapbook *R* was awarded the 2015 Keystone Chapbook Poetry Prize at Seven Kitchens Press and published in Summer 2016.

Thank you to the magazines and journals where the following poems have been published in various forms:

"Proud Flesh," *So to Speak Journal*, Spring 2015

"Unwash Me in Front of My Grandfather," *Duende*, Spring 2015

"Pornography," *VoiceCatcher*, Summer 2015

"The Deer in December" and "Phonetics," *Cascadia Review*, Fall 2015

"Preparation of the Mummy: An Introduction," "Mad Scientist," "Monsters in the Closet," and "Succubus," *Menacing Hedge*, Fall 2015

"Aliens," *Fjords Review—Women's Edition*, Fall 2015

"Blocked Memories" and "The Gospel According to Jane Doe," *Synesthesia Journal*, Fall 2015

"Another Girl Goes Down" and "Packing List for the Damaged," *Siren*, September 2015

"Good and Evil," "Villain Song for Medusa," and "Villain Song for the Penguin," *Arsenic Lobster*, Issue 39, Winter 2015

"Hymen," *Chiron Review*, Winter 2015

"An Experiment," *A Quiet Courage*, December 29, 2015

"Reading Rousseau at the Seattle Women's Clinic," *Rust and Moth*, Winter 2015

"Denial Is a Cavefish," "Ex Post Facto," and "Fraktur: A House Blessing," *Thirteen Myna Birds*, Spring 2016

"Body Mods for the Teenage Girl" and "The Cuckoo Clock," *The Fem*, March 2016

"American Eagles: A Totem," *Pilgrimage Magazine*, The Injustice Issue, Summer 2016

"Brunnhilde's Solo," *Rose Red Review*, July 2016

"Gather Round My Dinner Table," *Uppagus*, August 2016

"When Aedos Crawled In," *White Stag*, The Neogoddesses Anthology, Fall 2016

"Naming Ceremony," *Dying Dahlia Review*, October 2016

"Suicide 1979," *MARY: A Journal of New Writing*, December 2016

"Jackson Pollock Paints Pammy T's Daddy," *Unbroken Journal*, January 2017

Dedication

I extend deep gratitude to my MFA mentors at the Rainier Writing Workshop at Pacific Lutheran University, David Biespiel and Greg Glazner. David helped me examine the body closely. Greg helped convince me of my own talent.

Many thanks go to poet and MFA director, Rick Barot, and poet and teacher, Lia Purpura, for supporting *Villain Songs* and singing its praises.

Thank you to my poetry teachers: Kevin Goodan, Holly Hughes, Peggy Schumacher, and JT Stewart. You put the poetry wind in my sails.

Thank you to my beautiful aunt and uncle in Germany, Adelheid and Norbert Brandt. I am so blessed to find you and write our family story

Thank you to my RWW sister-wives Carol McMahon, Colleen Rain, and Cate Gable, for your tireless friendship, love, support, belief, and care while I birthed these poem-babies.

Thank you to my extended family circle of love and writerly support: Holly Burton Richart, Shadow ManyWhales, Judy Burchill, The Edman Family, Carol Hughes, Shelly Barnard, The Barnard Family, The Nelson Family, Denise Kumani Gantt, Keely Bowers, Lorin Bowman Hosmer, Zoe Zolbrod, Alice Anderson, Norbert Krapf, Rondau Duranseau, Greg Jensen, Rachel Barton, Laura Peterson, and Chelsey Clammer.

Thank you to the Tacoma Arts Commission, Hedgebrook, and MoonPath Press.

Thank you to my editor, Lana, for her care and thoughtful envisioning of my art, my writing, the book's cover, and the book lay-out.

Thank you most of all to my love, Brett Edman. This book is for you. For always.

For my niece, Casey

Table of Contents

Preparation of the Mummy: An Introduction | 3
Jane Doe | 7
Brunnhilde's Solo | 8
Hymen | 9
The Gospel According to Jane Doe | 10
Villain Song After the Burned Lady | 11
Finger Quotes | 13
I Did Not Like the Men | 14
Phonetics | 15
Jumping Beans | 16
Pornography | 17
Mad Scientist | 18
Monsters in the Closet | 19
The Great Temptation | 20
The Incarnations of Santa Claus | 21
Good and Evil | 22
Denial Is a Cavefish | 23
A Reconciliation | 24
Succubus | 25
Groomed | 26
The Changeling | 27
Yellow-bellied Parakeet | 28
Unwash Me in Front of My Grandfather | 29
When Aedos Crawled In | 30
Suicide 1979 | 32
American Eagles: A Totem | 33
Blocked Memories | 36
Villain Song for Ilsebill | 37
Villain Song for Medusa | 38

Villain Song for the Penguin | 39
Aliens | 40
Another Girl Goes Down | 41
Jackson Pollock Paints Pammy T's Daddy | 42
Burn Barrel | 43
Holes | 44
Reading Rousseau at the Seattle Women's Clinic | 46
Naming Ceremony | 47
An Experiment | 48
The Mortician Considers | 49
Packing List for the Damaged | 50
Body Mods for the Teenage Girl | 51
The Cuckoo Clock | 52
Amphibians | 54
Ex Post Facto | 56
Proud Flesh | 57
The Deer in December | 58
My Satchel | 59
Perverted Karma | 60
Gather Round My Dinner Table | 61
Fraktur: A House Blessing | 62

About the Author | 65

VILLAIN SONGS

Preparation of the Mummy: An Introduction

"They tried to bury us.
  But we were seeds."
    —*Proverb*

You may save my innards, silent in their poisoned stasis.
Trade my uterus for amulets. Freeze me in mausoleum
    diorama
of liver stomach intestine lungs. Pose them with my quiet
    tongue

in canopic jars. Still I breathe the truth. The holy lobes
of my brain will be shook loose. All complex matter and
    proof
labeled refuse. The memories tapped out by an iron hook

and pulled down through my nose. I feel them slipping,
piece by piece. The mess blessed and secreted away.
Removal by the highest priest in a jackal mask.

My life was never magnificent as much as an elaboration
of steps—a test by more officious names to carry me out
of the world. But I chiseled myself here in hieroglyph.

Rinse me. Salt me. Wrap me. There is no Nile pure
    enough.
There is no spice fragrant enough. There is no bandage
    tight
enough to tamp out this legacy. Now it is written.

My bones crack beneath the death straps. My marrow
    steams
itself out to dust. To dust and air and light. Flip the scarabs
to see my dried eyes. You will find holes where they fly.

Study the sarcophagus etched with poems.
Regretless upon my coffin stone, I dared speak.
The dead spread of me stuffed with papyrus leaves.

*In the dark times,
will there also be singing?
Yes, there will also be singing.
About the dark times.*

—Bertolt Brecht

Jane Doe

Originally I hail
from Pennsylvania
deer hunters.
My father named
his first rifle:
Meat in the Pot.

To be a female
among such creatures
was like the slow doe
in open meadow
who blundered off:
A perfect shot.

Brunnhilde's Solo

Uncrushed on the velvet
fainting sofa, I rise in flash

and glint. The evening is gowned
for gold lament. I'm a German

opera braided with heavy blonde
plaits and tragi-songs of parting

and longing. But I'm secretly
detached. My performance is

metallic. I'm steadying my head
to ignite the stage. Helmuted

in halo spotlight, whole notes
immolate my golden throat

with verse and flame. Heaven's
about to blow. And God? He's dead.

Hymen

The tulle veil
was bone china
white and thin.
A breakable wisp.

It was fleeting.
Mother snapped
shots of it
on Sundays.

I sat in the family
rocking chair
in the unused room
with ankles crossed.

Swirl feel
under the skirt
of my church dress.
It lived there.

A lace sash
tied off
access to
the pure me.

My holiness
sewn
delicate
as an eyelet.

The Gospel According to Jane Doe

When Christ popped
the seal on my tomb,
I was still doomed.

There was no Lazarus.
No Gabriel. No angels.
Not even God,

save the men of God
with holy orders, standing
in their officious cloaks

at the site. Dirty joking
uncles and the friends
of the fathers, the host

spirits who came upon me
early like pre-puberty. Oily,
slow and ruinous. Their pious

Easter hymns, snaking
under my grave-clothes,
pimpling the skin.

Villain Song After the Burned Lady

My testament
was a test said the guest

speaker the burned lady
when she preached

to our school about surviving
disaster and pranksters

who gifted her at an overpass
with a vat of acid

It was random
I was random

I can't recall her name
since I saw the injury first

and whispered with friends
about her bad wig

But what did high school know
way back then

if a body meet a body
turned inside out

in the auditorium
back to class

fast forward
thirty years

I still see that molten hole
a keloid kewpie doll

face now my own
kind of mess

a message turned on itself
these poems a fire burning

to reach the other side
of my teeth

Finger Quotes

On vacation in a hotel room
with two queen-sized beds
my sister laid out on her back

on one bed and my dad went down
next to her. He laughed about
what the neighbors would think.

He joked and whispered
something about perverts
to my sister. So, I turned

to leave. Then she called
after me, *I guess nobody
can have any fun since you got—*

With two air claws each
she scraped and re-scraped
the word *"molested"* for me.

I Did Not Like the Men

When they whistled at my mother
I was four years old the first time

we walked holding hands
on the sidewalk they called down

crude obscenities
from the top of a tall building

I never heard such caterwauling
Ignore them Ignore them she said

But it goes on even after she is dead
happening at my bus stop

on the way to school
in downtown Seattle

beautiful Santa Barbara
at the airport so rude

so juicy mmmm hey fat ass
bitch why can't you smile for me?

Phonetics

In this land my mother became my mutter.
Or a mommy could be a moody depending
on how you called for her. Brother was brooder.
A sister was in-cester. Or in-sweater. I unfastened
myself to adapt and pulled new names out.

See, I was eight, but no meant nine. Then mine
was diner. This strange new tongue tying
German to my English. I learned by marrying
words I already carried to strangers. Linked
them up like plump sausages. This gets wurst.

Red hots became knocks. Brats. Bloods
and maids. This is my nightshirt. See?
Yes, I could. Opa had me touch it anyway.
Pullover was bowl of her. Dog was hunt.
But hand was still hand in this land.

Jumping Beans

At first, I thought
they were magic.

Like hard candy,
I wanted to suck them.

I wanted to believe my Opa
pulled them from his pocket

as a treat. But he ridiculed me
and dropped the dull beans

in a pot on the old gas stove.
So I guessed they were bones.

Until I saw one move.
I realized the creatures

inside the pod were alive.
He turned up the fire

and held my arm. Kept me
there, close by, to get it hot.

He made me watch
as the brown pods lurched,

hurt and tossed themselves
to pilled stillness

across his burning,
black kitchen pot.

Pornography

Excitable
some animals are just born that way

the spotty mutt with mange
my Opa named Schlocky

the first German word I learned
it means trashy think cheap cheap

cheap like the kitchen parakeet
that old yellow thing

always around did not much sing
but jerked its head 90 degrees

when my mother dragged up
an old metal washtub to bathe me

openly it would swing swing
swing itself back and forth

I smelled cigarettes
while he acted busy

in the same room but
watched me sideways

Mad Scientist

There were many possibilities
at the butcher shop in Bayreuth.
They hung dozens of pigs
whole, strung up by their feet.
Thick legs. Pink skin. Blue-milk

gaze. My Opa browsed around
the freezing aisles, hooking a look
at a sow with the plumpest rump.
He fingered its ribs. How many ways
can you break down a fresh pig?

Monsters in the Closet

The ghouls were girls in bags
of stag mags stashed in the corner.

One mothership gashed open
a centerfold spread: Two-legged

creatures with grins and blonde
heads. Many-eyed splendors bounced

out. Shame split the earth apart
in the dark crotch of that closet,

so when the devil came he did right swift.
He pulled the thingy string swinging

from a bulb overhead. That naked
curse lit him up for you like a new idea.

The Great Temptation

like Satan led Christ
    I was led

up the mountain
    to his armchair

stopping at the crest
    we rocked together

to marvel the vista
    then the tongue-feel

he pled smoothly
    curled around me

all this he hissed
    it's yours

The Incarnations of Santa Claus

Jolly ole Saint Nick
with a shepherd's stick.

Black Peter
and his hazel switch.

Who will shape-shift
for the timeless gimmick?

My *Christkindl*
was an old school pimp.

He wrapped his schtick
in whiskers and gifts.

Good and Evil

The bad dreams played like Saturday morning cartoons
where super heroes had hard ons and the Hamburglar
shushed me to come sit on his lap or a stormy blonde Thor
crushed the clouds my angry Norseman splitting heaven

apart I opened my girl thighs and throbbed to animations
of him pummeling villages and mountains on the hunt
under my covers his thunder and rock hammer striking up
what I already knew by then a girl like me had it coming.

Denial Is a Cavefish

Peculiar mother
species of the North
European cave.

From freshwater
lineage, now trans-
parent and eyeless.

Is she mutated
and cryptic?
Or just adaptive?

She swims
eternally forward
in the pool

pitch black,
and she never
looks back.

A Reconciliation

When the tantes arrived oblivious
with their air kisses and teased hair,
I frisked their drunk husbands. Uncles

who wore their white bellies swollen
in tight shirts over leather belts like Stöllen
loaves. Lounging low in armchairs, they called

for my company. So I laughed at their jokes.
I coaxed them for treats. It was a restitution.
The gentleman's agreement. I dug pocket deep

to appease us each by reaching in
to pull out hard penny candies or
wrap my hand around a tangerine.

Succubus

I saw how pinup girls pose.
I was very young,

I confess. And on my sister
we focused a pretend lens.

Her repose in shirtlessness;
I recall the strawberry

nevus. A tiny birth-
mark on child chest.

Something so innocent
yet, I've grown it

to a smudge.
A puncture wound.

What did I arouse
in the marring?

It crosses my mind
often, that moment

a terrible exposure
lit past childhood aperture

to shape my adult mind's
eye. The shame,

a refraction.
Stain on me.

Groomed

Still, I sang love songs
for him. I ate sliced calf liver
smothered in sharp mustard.
I nipped spiced liqueur
before the tortes. Snorted
pinches of a tingly, brown
magic dust. What a rush
of his snuff! To be so high
but so young. But I didn't know
any better. I loved him. Of course
I petted the smooth *Singvogel*
out of its cage while he cooked
worse things up in the kitchen,
while he planned and cooed.
I carried on and on for my Opa,
Ick Liebe Dick! Ick Liebe Dick!
to make my way through.

The Changeling

At Christmas, Opa gave you a girl-doll
and signed it, *Christkindl*.

From the Christ Child.
It bore a likeness to you.

Curly brown hair. Green eyes
watching while you spoiled her.

You would always feel the hurt,
followed by the hollow. Searching

for something to satisfy. You fed her
a plastic milk bottle when you finished.

It was a kind of forgiveness.
When she cried and sipped, you tried

to return the things you stole
back into her hole.

Yellow-bellied Parakeet

Coward parakeet,
you were not a crowd
as much as a culprit.

Like my friend Shar
who said her sister feigned sleep
when her father crept in. My pet,

what did you see? Dirty
birds. Bed spread eagles.
He's lined our cage with titty

magazine pages. Oh strange
feathered bedfellow. My egg
Benedict. Godless yet

perched omniscient
in the high corner, wingless
you swing silent behind bars

all these years. And I know just
what tale you should tweet.
Your villain song squawks

my secret free.

Unwash Me in Front of My Grandfather

Pull the washcloth out
of this small dirty place.
Unclean my pits.

Unrub my thighs. Mother,
drag this all back
through milky time

up the cold tub-side.
Back to mid air. Suspend it
there. Leave me unfoamed.

Get me unwet. Hold me
dry, placed in your lap. Then
lift me high. Toward the light.

Unnuded. Refolded. Perfect
and clean. Fresh backward
toward the linen closet.

Stop the water now,
from running over me.
Use both handles.

Turn them off.
Turn him off.
Turn this back.

When Aedos Crawled In

Zeus designed me
        without enough humility.
                So he called upon Aedos.

                Daughter of shame.
        Daughter of modesty.
Persona of reverence.

Persona of backwardness.
        She enters a human body
                from the rear. Wriggling

                in, head first. She belly-
        slid along. Reptilian,
with tiny foot grips.

What dark shaft
        did she ascend?
                The higher she climbed,

        the tighter it went.
        I grew around her
in a dark suffocation

of sludge-wet breath
        until her lungs breathed
                in rhythmic time

                with mine. She assumed
        the overwhelm
and toxic fumes

of my secrets.
>How far deep
>>did she ever get? When

>>my cheeks burn scarlet
>red, I know she stirs there
yet, in my utmost pit.

Suicide 1979

That summer I chose suicide first—

The name of the drink where you mix a shot
of liquor from every bottle at the mini-bar,
because you don't care what will happen.

That summer my parents broke up, we flipped
quarters to decide which one to live with.

That summer I realized my thighs
will always rub together
since the tread marks burned into me.

That summer of *Flowers in the Attic*
a book that confirmed
Cathy's older brother began to molest.

That summer of birthday cake. At Debbie Smith's
slumber party every girl shaved her legs
but me. All of them brown, vanilla, and pink-
kneed, new scoops of Neapolitan ice cream.

That summer they asked, *Truth or Dare?*
So I said, *Dare me*, and drank down a cup
of self-murder when given the choice,
then slept all night in my jeans.

American Eagles: A Totem

I.

It was decades too late
When the government demolished
The Tekakwitha Orphanage.

Old Native American brothers
Stood with their aging sisters
To watch the wrecking ball

Crash down

An empty holy place
Where they arrived scared
Birds to be white-educated,

But all left raped.
A Dakota expression for 'child'
Wakan injun—they too are sacred.

II.

What breach sound
Does the eagle squeak?
Is it a screech or a squawk?
A shriek or a cluck or a clique?
Or an ick ick ick—Dear God
Is it just silence coming
from the Papoose House
Nursery where Catholics stood
Native children nude?

Day after night
Day after night

A Godhead invitation
To the Black Masquerade.
When the good Father
Blessed the brown chicks
To eat of his body
They held sparrow breath
In the spread open folds
Of dark-winged robes
Once the nuns swooped in.

III.

The crawl spaces
Collapsed. The altar
Faltered, then fell.
The dying rooms
Dropped all walls
Brick by brick
To Dakota dust
While the siblings

Beheld three eagles

Circling the sky.
They all knew
It was spirit
Coming to call
When the birds
Dove and rose
Dove and rose—
Up from the rubble
To carry their
Own back home.

Blocked Memories

—After Katherine Poyner-Del Vento

Forgetting is white.
A mattress stripped.
My dad draped bed linens
over the furniture in my room,
so bereft my mother packed us
up that winter and left.

And me, I never could tell
the poor man it happened then.
I tucked the secret beneath my body.
Silence fell across me like down.
For forty years I have slept
on it. Blank as a sheet till now.

Villain Song for Ilsebill

The fisherman's wife
wished to be king.

Not princess.
Not queen,

but pope.
Or world ruler

orchestrating ocean,
revolving sun and moon.

What woman wouldn't
beg for that new boon?

Ho, the grand fish-prince boiled
in his perfect blue man sea

Then he stuck Ilsebill in a pigsty
to humble such thinking.

The husband hands
back on her

with their fish
stink.

Villain Song for Medusa

Sometimes the green monster in me
still believes it's a bud-pink maiden.

When I half-close my lids to dream,
the snakes uncoil from my crown.

They swish down like golden hair.
Again, my skin is young. I am fair.

I trick myself to hold love's stare
with this bloodstone glare.

I do not blame the boys now
for being afraid of what they see.

But what other choice rose out
from heaven for me? My goddess

first-bloom plucked in Poseidon's sea.
His seduction, my miserable ripening.

Villain Song for the Penguin

I'm one cold, vocal bird.
A strange Arctic runt.

When he fished his hand
straight up my chickie cunt

he split me apart. Black in
back. Stark white affront.

That crack opened
like smooth dorsal wings.

Never meant to fly,
I will never fly.

But I can sing.

Aliens

Laurie the cool babysitter offered me some coke
at 12 years old when we went to see Spielberg's E.T.
at the drive-in. I laid across the warm hood of her car
and escaped into the big screen draping the night stars
that splintered out from the backdrop like a windshield
sucker punched. Like a broken family of constellations.
When the spaceship left E.T. alone on earth he drank
beer he found and got the poor boy he loved drunk.
Sometimes childhood is an attachment to threatening
life forms. A gravitation toward the ladies room
at intermission. A line of blow cut across a commode.
The comet burn flaring up. I grew a tail and taller. I grew
two heads. I flew too. My white hot spirit spinning off
lost in space. Something better out there. I believed.

Another Girl Goes Down

Into a ditch. Maybe she hit a rock. Maybe she did not pay close attention. Maybe she's only twelve whereas you're an F-10. An American truck with a large bed. Used to haul things like lumber. Dogs. Men. Men who ride wild in mongrel packs and play air guitar or smoke up their cigarettes. Men who know how to disintegrate the world from a Ford window. Their ashtray. A dump site shoveled down deep just for them and the ground opened just for her.

Jackson Pollock Paints Pammy T's Daddy

There is no plan just subject here I am the drip the
smear the nanny that circles the room chasing after tiny
Pammy T it is a canvas it is a kitchen I am a chicken I
walk the perimeter so wide so white so wolfen with Mr
T peckish at center table but I am a chicken little chick
out in an open pen he spreads like a newspaper open
as the mouth of a thick mug I fill the space steam can't
escape fixed there as coffee and cream drawn up to two
lips wide as his thighs in a blue bathrobe sky open as
Cody, Wyoming where Pollock grew up you never saw
land expand like those miles of grain colored plains
in the mountain west when you assess canvas that
monstrous you can look into the light peep past the
blinding vastness of a thing a burbling dark negative
space is what breaks through the thread holes pricked
in a seam to be a painting to be an elegy O elegies for
nannies elegies for the good fathers some-where elegies
for pubic hair O elegies for those of us who grieve what
can never be unseen

Burn Barrel

Wild dogs are taking over this place. Their horns play Dixie. As if. Meanwhile the men are mean. Once I watched my dad skin a pregnant hare. You grew up driving trucks here. Trucks sweet with hemis and chassis. Words in machine parts. That language is lost on me. Brian something. I can't remember his last name. We drank Bacardi by the bottle in the cab of my Cabriolet. Then the hickeys. Glug. Glug. Simply the thirsty, simple boys. The Scotts. The Robs. The Mikes. Sometimes they come running back when you call. Sometimes they don't. Love is a bitch. You say you listen to metal. Let me guess. The Very Beast of Dio or Ozzy's Bark at the Moon? They hang in packs. I'm not sure what a crankshaft seems like. Breed symptoms include manufactured porch, muddy lawn, muscle car on blocks. My dad and his beagle could run a rabbit in the woods all day long. Relentlessly, my mom sliced onions and boiled water in a pot for stew on the old stove. You pace the kitchen waiting around. The air here suffocates you. Always something horrible burning out back.

Holes

I remember feeling the hollow
swallow me whole again
in college one day
when a strange man
on the crowded number 7 bus
stood over me in the aisle
and pushed his pelvis
into my shoulder
every time we hit a bump.
He pumped it
spasmodically
while pretending to read
the Seattle Times.
His carelessness
overwhelmed me
while he looked away
but kept at it
like a garden hose
trying to fill a bud vase.
I thought I imagined it.
Then I thought it was
an accident. I realize now
I was simply an opportunity.
I was an empty space
to encase himself,
even though I had a job to go to,
a big trig test on Wednesday.
I was the zero-sum. A young
number adding up to nothing.
And my shoulder didn't count
for as much as how I was meant

to accommodate him. A lucky break.
An opening. His rightful place
to bury something.

Reading Rousseau at the Seattle Women's Clinic

Henri had 'no other teacher
but nature.' I recalled that factoid
from an art history class while peaking

thick with narcotics in the clinic bed
then they scotch-taped me to the ceiling
in his poster-sized jungle print.

The safe place for banished PYTs
ripe with uglifruit, there I learned
a woman leaves *The Virgin Forest*

much the same way she came in.
I laid across the forest's plush green
canvas. My own foliage, shaved down

the night before. Smooth palm leaves
split open in jungle book narrative
where the shadow doctor conflicted

beneath my uterine sun—
part man part beast.
Then the thunder.

And it was busted asunder.
And then it was over.
Blood orange fruition

of the smallest, wild hope
crawled out of me for five days
in broken shells and poked yolk.

Naming Ceremony

Secret burial plot
Dug ever deep
Behind the maiden eye.

I come here often
To wonder and pray.
I always wanted

To keep you.
What name can I say
For seven weeks?

Pink Teardrop
Love Shrimp
Swimming Lee

Golden Tadpole
Wild Yonder
Bluet Elegy

An Experiment

In 1944 studies were conducted
at the Dachau concentration camp
to make sea water drinkable.
It never was. The sick Gypsies
so thin and dehydrated
from thirst. Observant staff
took notes watching the prisoners
crawl the fresh-mopped floors
to lick up the wet.

I called my Opa once in 1994
some years after my mother died
to confront him for what he did.
I never could. In broken German
I deciphered my Oma was dead.
Bad heart, he offered in static
overseas. *I love you. Come home
to me.* And I believed him all over
again. *I will try*, I wept.

The Mortician Considers

I might paint you in voodoo
a sugar skull groom
with his lipless grimace

father zombie
do a smoky eye
á la kohl

apple of yours
never mine
your fists kissed

while they rest now
father death wish
in a peaceful fold

but I just might
pose them calloused
at my mother's throat

your legacy open-faced
a necklace of cremains
decorum in memoriam

charms for my chain

Packing List for the Damaged

she-wolf eyes
snake pupils
ear of lynx

kodiak paws
roach thorax
can of kerosene

tail of newt
spare wishbone
panther claws

bottle of bitters
lithium
tiger balm

schmear of snail
rabbit foot
bull's heartbeat

stretch of tentacle
turtle shell
wild monkey screech

Body Mods for the Teenage Girl

Grind shark tooth smile

Attach thunder bolt thighs

Braid hair with boas

Stitch eyes open wide

Pierce kryptonite lip ring

Weave barbed wire skin

Grow pin cushion heart

Lace sharp tongued Keds

The Cuckoo Clock

When I was a girl
I wanted to live
inside of one.

A wooden, small
place to hold me.
I was in love

with its bird
face. I imagined us
married. The dream

of domesticity. Keeping
house à la bric-a-brac
or conversation piece.

But time has told
what makes them tick.
More machinations

than magic. Dark
pastoral scenes
and a stiffness

crowns the eaves.
Clockmakers all carve
the same male game

in their overhang.
Reared buckhorns
and alpha beasts—

They rule the ornate
roost. And it's a heavy
pull on me. Those two

coniferous strung
weights dangling
their gonadal hang.

Amphibians

The French Creek
        salamanders surfaced black
and fast. Like a dark mood.

Like my mother's
        impatience. My father's rage.
I terrorized too

and swung a young one
        till he broke free of his tail
to be rid of me. How

does one escape
        their fate? Regenerate
tissue, tail, retina

of eye or tongue?
        This heart of newt
is brute and old.

It pumps cold
        family blood.
But still I try

to swim back
        to what was good—
from tadpole

to tiny egg.
        To jellied unload.
To the wet dream

of my possibility
        before those two toads
got hold of me.

Ex Post Facto

At which time
He was appointed

Acting head
Of the doll hospital

To govern the broken
Celluloid committee

Of ill, nude dollies and all
Their turtle-mark parts.

They winked once for, Yes.
They winked twice for, Forget.

Before that
He played a doctor.

And before that,
A patient, we suspect.

Proud Flesh

I've spun galaxies of new red cells
into one dark, clotted Mars. Woven raw
memory to keloidal scars in proliferation
to raised grotesqueness. What existed
was an injury, then an overcompensation.
An ambling. My limp of years.

But I will only carry the living wound
to here. This burned out star. Now I take it,
like heirloom plates, and break it apart.
Crush the taboo. Examine the fragments
dead pan. Then smash it again.
To be a new thing. To be kintsukuroi.
How the Japanese celebrate the broken

by weaving it back together in mosaic,
with love's molten thread. A true life
beginning from such sacred, golden joinery.
All my loss laid out in a universal strategy
of shards so refined they will glitter
and shine a new path. That I may walk away
from myself, across the sky's fine brilliance.

The Deer in December

Since your death,
my hard heart softens

in small measures.
When the deer steps

down into my yard,
he minces his feet

along my frosted garden
so tentative,

so carefully now.
As if you are sorry.

Dear brown-eyed, remorseful
creature still coming around

for a daughter's vestiges.
My forgiveness parcels itself out

in pinchfuls of seeds.
I let you feed

on my pale winter
kale and weeds.

My Satchel

I left many things behind
to come back. I orphaned my doll
with shiny brown hair. Returned
schokolade candies that finished

like rum. I extinguished my Opa
there in a tiny, blue box of snuff.
I brushed the whole year off—
A dandruff. I let the bad fall down

where it landed with the beautiful
too. A golden leather satchel I loved
had a long, thick shoulder strap
and metal snap flap. Such a smart bag

I couldn't bring. But sometimes
I peer back into it, pulling out dark
tobacco and Kinder egg treats.
My parents too, dead but still

mine. Living among these other
fragile trinkets. Our family secrets
I keep locked here. My heart,
a deep, hidden pocket.

Perverted Karma

My mother passed down
your 18 carat pinky ring.

An heirloom showpiece.
Thick-built manly thing

boasting a square-cut garnet
that crowned dead center.

But I sold the gold
to an old fogey

at a curio shop.
He pressed and pushed

his thumb clean through
the rear end

until the gem broke free.
Then dropped

your popped cherry
in my palm for keeps.

Gather Round My Dinner Table

Come, Aunt #1/ Lover of screw-drivers/ Thrice spliced divorcee/ Rosacea tattooed/ Yes, Mother/ You who feigns sleep often/ Titmouse/ Heirloom for the Christmas tree/ Sit now, Grand Mal/ Old Bertha canals/ Eyes wide shut/ AKA—The accomplice/ Join in, Cousin #5/ A fluffer/ Accepts small coins and gifts/ Paves way/ Welcome, Only Sister/ Conjoined twin winner/ Duplicitous/ Sips from poisoned well/ Oh Naturally, Me/ Black scribe/ Stands with fists and fits/ The pressure washer/ Go! Little Niece/ Do not eat here/ Escaped chance/ Bargaining chip/ Our thing with wings

Fraktur: A House Blessing

The afterward, a kind
of commemoration

dinner. Grief pulling
out his empty chair

from table's head.
The soiled linen

of what is said and done
lifted from us.

Carcass of dead bird
just a bone cage

staging the center
plate. Picked clean

of innards and dark heart,
his quiet, broken neck

already squirreled away
for our soup the next day.

About the Author

Tammy Robacker graduated with her MFA in Creative Writing, Poetry from the Rainier Writing Workshop at Pacific Lutheran University in 2016. Tammy won the 2015 Keystone Chapbook Prize for her manuscript, "R". Tammy is a Hedgebrook writer-in-residence award winner (2010). She published her first collection of poetry, *The Vicissitudes*, in 2009 (Pearle Publications) with generous support from a Tacoma Artist Initiative Grant award (2009). Tammy's poetry has appeared in *Alyss, FRiGG, Tinderbox, Menacing Hedge, Chiron Review, VoiceCatcher, Duende, So to Speak, Crab Creek Review, WomenArts*, and many more. Tammy is a poet, teacher, and professional writer living with her fiancé in Oregon. Visit: TammyRobacker.com

www.ingramcontent.com/pod-product-compliance
Lightning Source LLC
Chambersburg PA
CBHW021450080526
44588CB00009B/773